[THOMAS TRYON]

A DISCOURSE
of the
Causes, Natures and *Cure*
of
Phrensie, Madness or *Distraction*

from

A TREATISE OF DREAMS & VISIONS

[1689]

Introduction by
MICHAEL V. DEPORTE

WILDSIDE PRESS

INTRODUCTION

Thomas Tryon was born in Gloucestershire the son of a tiler, and had only a year of formal schooling. At six, when he had barely learned to distinguish the letters of the alphabet, his father set him to work carding and spinning wool. Tryon worked hard and soon became an excellent spinner, but he was drawn to the freer, healthier life of the shepherds whose flocks he would offer to tend in his spare hours. After several years Tryon persuaded his father to buy him some sheep and allow him to take to the fields. It was while wandering with his flocks, he recalls in his *Memoirs*, that he first began to contemplate "the vast usefulness of Reading."[1] He bought a primer, and with the help of his fellow shepherds and a more literate villager (to whom he gave a sheep in return for lessons), taught himself to read and write. By the time he was eighteen he had tired of herding sheep; he wanted to travel, and deciding to sell his flocks set out for London. On reaching the city he prudently bound himself apprentice to a hatter and settled down to learn the trade that was to make him his fortune. Tryon was no ordinary apprentice. He worked eighteen hour days to earn extra money so that he might buy books and hire himself tutors. He read widely in the natural sciences and in hermetic lore. He was particularly drawn to medicine and to astrology, which he respected as a study that sought to understand "the Method of God's Government in Nature, and Administration of the World" (pp. 22-23), and which he felt had been too rashly discredited on account of the rapacious and ignorant charlatans who abused it. Some five years after beginning his apprenticeship Tryon underwent a kind of religious conversion or rather, since his religious convictions were already strong, an intensification of belief. "The blessed Day-Star of the Lord," he writes, "began to arise and shine in my Heart and Soul, and the Voice of Wisdom continually and most powerfully called upon me for Separation and Self-denial" (p. 26). Always of a sober and thoughtful disposition he now became increasingly ascetic in his habits. He gave up eating meat and determined to take no drink except water, a resolution he broke from time to time owing to the "inward temptations of the Evil Genius," but which on the whole he kept to with a firmness characteristic of his tenacity of purpose and indifference to received opinion:

> ... some may be apt here to interpose, and say, Why all this Singularity? And that it is ridiculous to run Retrograde from all our Neighbours, and what advantage found you in it? To this I Answer, That I found this abstemious clean way of living in Innocency, mightily to fit and qualifie me for the contemplation of our great Creator, and of his wonderful Works in Nature; for by throughly cleansing the outward Court of the Terrestrial Nature, and thereby raising the power of the outward Senses at the same time as it were, it opens the Window of the inward Senses of the Soul, so that they become clear-sighted, and can discern and distinguish between the good and evil Principles ... (pp. 29-31).

Tryon was forty-eight before, having an "inward Instigation to Write and Publish something to the World," he turned author. During the years following his arrival in London he had prospered in the hatting trade, taken several voyages to Barbadoes for the sake of expanding his business, and "married a sober young Woman, but of a contrary Sentiment to mine, as to Diet." Not surprisingly, his first works concern the preservation of health and character through diet. Tryon propounded his dietary laws with great zeal and they came to have considerable influence. Benjamin Franklin read *The Way to Health* at sixteen and became an ardent Tryonist until one day, being sorely tempted to eat fish and remembering that when the fish had been cut open a smaller fish had been found in its belly, he put his scruples aside with the thought if the big fish had a right to the little fish surely he had a right to it.[2]

Tryon had the enthusiasm for study and hypothesizing of a self-educated man, and soon proceeded to air his views on other subjects. Were it not for the religious piety evidenced in nearly all his work, one might almost see in him a living counterpart of Walter Shandy. Like Walter he amassed enough wealth through trade to enable him to devote his later years to philosophical speculations as wide-ranging as they often are peculiar. Above all like Walter, he believed that "an ounce of a man's own wit was worth a tun of other peoples."[3] "Whoever doubts or mistrusts, and goes out of himself, and wanders abroad for a Director," Tryon warns, "is in danger to be captivated by the Clouds of Darkness, or fettered in the Chains of Tradition and Custom" (p. 36/54).[4] "It ought," he says elsewhere in the Memoirs, "to be a Man's chief Pleasure, to set his Light on the Top of an Hill, that all may receive the benefit of it, if they will" (p. 16/50). Judging from his writings, and he wrote some sixteen books, this was indeed Tryon's chief pleasure. His pet theories have to do with dietetics, but he has theories also regarding astrology and the education of children, the treatment of slaves and the political situation in Europe, ways of amassing riches and ways of achieving mystical revelation, the significance of dreams and the causes of madness.

A Discourse of the Causes, Natures and Cure of Phrensie, Madness or Distraction was published as an appendix to a much longer work entitled A Treatise of Dreams and Visions [1689]. Of the Treatise itself little need be said here. Tryon had been fascinated with dreams since his earliest years when, as a young boy, he had two dreams which left a life-long impression. In one, God appeared, showed him the "Kingdom of Love and the Kingdom of Darkness," and then talked to him in a reassuring and loving manner. In the other, he was scourged by the Devil. These dreams both strengthened his resolve to live virtuously and convinced him that in dreams one might commune with heavenly or infernal powers. He explains in his Memoirs that throughout his adult life he not only tried to put each waking hour to the best use, but tried as well to take "all lawful Advantages" of his hours of repose "by minding and having regard to the Visitations and Communications of good Angels in [his] Dreams, and Nocturnal Representations to the wakeful Soul, while the bodily and outward Senses were suspended from their Functions" (p. 53/71). Tryon does not maintain in the Treatise that all dreams arise from supernatural influences; he allows that other influences—temperament, diet, illness, daily events, the sign under which one was born—often predominate. Much that the *Treatise* contains can be found also in Philip Goodwin's more scholarly work, *The Mystery of Dreams, Historically Discoursed* (1658), though Tryon emphasizes to an unusual degree the means by which revelatory dreams may be cultivated. It is through wholesome, virtuous living, and "by *Lonesomeness, Retirement* and *Silence*, [that] the mind is made fine, and as it were loosened from the cords & perturbations of worldly affairs, and is therby the better prepared, and the more at leisure to receive the spiritual Gifts, and free Communications of the good Angels of God."[5]

Tryon included his *Discourse on Madness* as an appendix to the *Treatise* because he believed there was "an Affinity or Analogy between *Dreams* and *Madness*," that madness was a *"Watching* or *Waking Dream"* (p. 249). He was by no means alone in perceiving this connection. Writers of the period, because of their increasing association of unrestrained imagination with insanity, sometimes made use of the dream as an analogue of madness. In *Enthusiasmus Triumphatus*, for example, Henry More had observed that the real difference between dreaming and waking is not that in dreams men imagine things they never do awake, but that in sleep they allow such fantasies to take the place of sensory experience. More suggests that if, when a man was awake, his imagination "were *so strong* as to bear it self against all the occursions and impulses of *outward* Objects, so as not to be broken, but to keep it self entire and in *equall* splendour and vigour with what is represented from *without*, and . . . the Party thus affected would not fail to take his own Imagination for a reall Object of Sense."[6] A man to whom this happened would, of course, be mad. More's aim in noting the resemblance of madness and dreams is essentially cautionary. Like Hobbes, or Swift, or Pope (who brilliantly exploits the relationship between dreams and madness in Book III of *The Dunciad* by having Cibber fall asleep in the lap of Dulness and dream his mad vision of a journey to the underworld), More wishes to show the folly of permitting imagination ascendancy over the senses, of allowing dream states to intrude upon objective reality.

Tryon's discussion of madness is cautionary in a somewhat different way. For him, too, madness results from a revolt of fancy whereby "the *Imaginative property* and *Soul's Power* becomes rampant, unbounded, or as it were without a Guide, and consequently such a Soul is unchain'd, or set at liberty from the dark Confinements of the grosser *Senses* and *Reason*, even as men in Dreams; for whatsoever in this state, is represented unto the Soul by the uncontrolable and unbounded Imagination, is essential unto them, whether it be good or evil" (p. 252). Tryon likens this condition to a civil war, the outcome of which is either anarchy or death. "The Soul," he says, in language half suggestive of "The Digression on Madness," "will no longer be confined to the Body and outward Senses, but either withdraws it self, and flings up the Reins of Government, and lets *Reason*, like a wilde Horse that hath cast off Bit and Bridle, and thrown his Rider, ramble confusedly whithersoever the Imagination shall hurry it; or else sometimes breaks off wholly all Commerce with the Body, and separates its self in Indignation, and so the Life its self is destroyed" (pp. 255-256). The crucial fact about madness for Tryon is thus loss of rational control. Ordinarily men submit their thoughts to the censure of judgment. They cannot stop thinking or easily determine what they will think; they can only decide which thoughts to express or act upon. In madness, however, the power of judgment is so vitiated that the barrier between thought and expression is removed; madmen do and say whatever comes into their heads. "For what wild, incoherent, absurd, ridiculous notions," Tryon writes, echoing a remark of Hobbes, "should we hear from the most serious people, if they should continually Speak, and form into words the various Imaginations, and Conceptions that do continually arise" in their brains (p. 259).[7]

At this point in the *Discourse* the argument diverges from the mainstream of contemporary psychology. Given what has been said one might next expect a further discussion of the care which should be taken to discipline the mind. But Tryon finds other lessons in madness. That men should lose control of their faculties is, he observes, perhaps not always so terrible a thing as is commonly supposed, because men are then rendered incapable of deception; "they appear naked, having no *Covering, Vail,* or *Figg-leaves* before them, to hide themselves in, and therefore they no longer remain under a Mask or Disguise, but appear even as they are, which is very rare to be known in any that retain their *Senses and Reason*" (p. 261). Madness reveals a man's true character, it becomes a test of personality. Seemingly upright, benevolent men may be exposed for the selfish, envious scoundrels they have all along been, whereas inwardly kindly but reserved men may be revealed as having in them far more good nature than anyone would have expected. To be a madman of the latter sort, where the "property of Friendliness" predominated, was to be a *"mad Innocent,"* and such madness, Tryon thought, had in it more of Christianity than what usually passed for sanity. "Sane" men, he argues, everyday commit acts of "greater *Madness* and Evil" than those confined. Who is to say that it is more extravagant for a man to think himself an emperor than for him to be conventionally ambitious, "sell his Liberty, and become a slave to the Lust and Capricio's of *Grandees* . . . in hopes of being one day made a great *man*" (pp. 263-264)? Is it worse for men to sit playing with straws than to become drunkards who "swallow down vast Estates at their *Throats,* and *Piss* away the Labours of their Ancestors against the *Wall*" (p. 264)? What then is the world, he asks, but a "great *Bedlam,* where those that are *more mad* lock up those that are *loss* [less]" (p. 266)?

Tryon's perspective on madness is at variance with that of his contemporaries, in part, because while he was anxious to check immorality, he set no premium on control of the irrational. Believing that truths of the deepest significance might be manifest in the "irrational" play of dreams, he was not prepared to discount the possibility of value in the erruption of that irrationality into waking life. Imagination is a faculty highly to be prized. Without imagination no idea could be brought to consciousness; what wonders it could perform, he muses, "if its mighty property were not captivated, darkned, and as it were chained in the Clouds of gross flesh" (pp. 260-261). Insanity, despite its terrors and perplexities, gives us a glimpse of those wonders.

Tryon's *Discourse* is a curious medley of acute observation and far-fetched hypothesis. On the one hand he is fond of riding his astrological hobby-horse, as when he attempts to classify mental illness according to the "seven Forms of Nature"—Saturnine, Jovial, Martial, Solar, Venereal, Mercurial, and Lunar—which may hold sway over the personality, or to show that madmen are especially subject to "Influences Coelestial." On the other hand, he offers a model for what happens to the mind in psychosis which, as Richard Hunter and Ida Macalpine have remarked, looks forward to modern psychologists who "use such terms as breakdown of ego function and reality testing."[8] His contention that madmen are compelled to express their every idea and feeling, though not providing for the fact that the insane do not always lose control over their thoughts, and may be capable of very considerable craft in their dealings with others, does afford insight into why the insane have in many ages commanded a certain awe. Madmen do not perceive things with the usual expectations and therefore do not see them in the usual way. Because they are free of ordinary inhibitions they report their experience in its absolute singularity. What they say may not at first make sense, yet often their remarks catch in the mind and remain, hinting at normally veiled significances. Throughout history there have been times when madmen were believed able to hit on truths denied to conventional intelligence. The Delphic priestesses were not only selected from among the mentally disturbed; they were further deranged by the fumes which rose up from the caverns beneath their temple, and delivered their prophecies in a state of frenzied incoherence. Though in the literature of the Renaissance madmen were typically used by writers to provoke laughter or horror, they were not always so used. Shakespeare's fools mingle nonsense with intuition; Lear's deepest understanding of his suffering, and of human suffering generally, comes to him in madness.

Though the *Discourse on Madness* and the *Treatise of Dreams* went through three editions there is little evidence that they had any immediate influence.[9] Tryon's appreciation for the innocence of madmen, his prizing of intuition and imagination over "rationality," could not be expected to gain much of a hearing in the 1690s; in this, as in other of his ideas, he was ahead, or at least out of, his times. But Tryon does anticipate the gradual resurgence of interest during the eighteenth century in madness as something more than a condition of ludicrous, pitiable, or abhorrent folly. This resurgence culminates in the frequent treatment of madness by writers of the romantic movement as a state of exhalted and uncommon awareness, and it can be traced in the changing fortunes of Don Quixote who, from being thought a character to inspire burlesques, a blockhead whose mishaps are a just and amusing consequence of preposterous obsessions, came to be admired for qualities closely approximating those of Tryon's mad innocents.[10]

Tryon's sympathetic interest in madness led him to take sharp issue with prevailing modes of therapy. He argued that to treat the insane by blood-letting or by drugging them with stupefactive medicines was at best useless, at worst apt to increase or prolong their sufferings. At a time when respectable doctors, the eminent Thomas Willis among them, condoned and even prescribed beatings for madmen to humble their pride, Tryon suggested that the greatest hope of cure lay in confining them to clean quarters, giving them wholesome food, and permitting them to be seen only by close, understanding friends.[11] It is a measure of Tryon's humanitarianism that nearly one-hundred years before official action was contemplated he should have called for the closing of Bedlam to the public. By the end of the seventeenth century Bedlam had become less a hospital than a human zoo in which visitors were free to taunt and insult the inmates and the keepers felt less responsibility to their charges than to the onlookers whom they served as guides. This raucous coming and going of spectators cruelly exacerbated the misery of the patients and defeated the very purpose of the institution. Tryon does cling to a belief in the salutary effects of purgatives and seems impressed by reports of Van Helmont's "ducking cure"—a primitive form of shock therapy whereby the patient was unexpectedly plunged into ice water—but for the main his views on the care of the insane are among the most enlightened of the period.

University of New Hampshire
Durham

NOTES TO THE INTRODUCTION

1. *Some Memoirs of the Life of Mr. Tho. Tryon, Late of London, Merchant* (London, 1705), p. 14. Subsequent references are given in the text.

2. *The Way to Health* (1691) which came to be Tryon's best known work, was a second edition of an earlier volume entitled *Health's Grand Preservative; or the Woman's Best Doctor* (London, 1682). Franklin reports this incident in his autobiography [ed. Leonard W. Labaree (New Haven: Yale Univ. Press, 1964), pp. 87-88].

3. *Tristram Shandy*, ed. James A. Work (New York: Odyssey Press, 1940), p. 147.

4. There is an error in the pagination of the *Memoirs* so that following p. 34 the numbering begins again at 1 and continues to 18 when, at what should be p. 53, the number is given as 35. Thus for references after p. 34 I have given first the printed number and then the correct number of the page.

5. *A Treatise of Dreams and Visions* (London, 1689), p. 234. Subsequent references are given in the text.

6. *Enthusiasmus Triumphatus*, 2nd. ed. (London, 1662), p. 4. This edition is reproduced as Augustan Reprint number 118.

7. Hobbes noted that "the most sober men, when they walk alone without care and employment of the mind, would be unwilling the vanity and Extravagance of their thoughts at that time should be publiquely seen: which is a confession, that Passions unguided, are for the most part meere Madnesse" [*Leviathan*, ed. A. D. Lindsay (New York: Dutton, 1950), p. 61].

8. *Three Hundred Years of Psychiatry 1535-1860* (London: Oxford University Press, 1963), p. 233.

9. A second edition appeared in 1691 entitled *Pythagoras his Mystick Philosophy reviv'd; or, the Mystery of Dreams unfolded*. Another edition bearing the original title was published as "The Second Edition" in 1695,

10. The evolution of attitudes toward Don Quixote and of the development of quixotic characters in English fiction is admirably discussed by Stuart Tave in *The Amiable Humorist* (Chicago: University of Chicago Press, 1960).

11. Willis speaks of the usefulness of beatings for subduing the passions of madmen in his *Discourse Concerning the Souls of Brutes* (London, 1679).

BIBLIOGRAPHICAL NOTE

The facsimile of *A Discourse of the Causes, Natures
and Cure of Phrensie, Madness or Distraction* is the
Appendix ("An Appendix Shewing the Cause of Madness; and Several Observables relating thereunto") to *A
Treatise of Dreams and Visions* [1689] and is
reproduced from a copy of the first edition (Shelf
Mark: *BF1075/T87) in the William Andrews Clark
Memorial Library. The total type-page (p.253) measures
127 x 65 mm.

A
TREATISE
OF
Dreams & Visions,

WHEREIN
Th· *Causes Natures* and *Uses* of
Nocturnal **Representations**, and
the **Communications** both of
Good and Evil **Angels**, as also
departed **Souls**, to Mankinde;

Are *Theosophically Unfolded* ; that is,
according to the *Word* of God, and
the *Harmony* of Created *Beeings*.

Night unto Night *sheweth* Wisdom, Psal. 19.2.

To which is added,
A **Discourse** of the *Causes*, *Natures*
and *Cure* of. *Phrensie*, *Madness*
or *Distraction*.

By **Philotheos Physiologus.**

AN APPENDIX

Shewing
The *Cause* of *Madness*;

AND

Several *Observables*
relating thereunto.

§. 1. THere being an **Affinity**
or Analogy between
Dreams and *Madness*, fo
that the underftanding of one will
fomewhat illuftrate the other; for
Madnefs feems to be a *Watching* or
Waking Dream; I have therefore
thought it might not be unfit to
fubjoyn here certain Confiderations
touching *Phrenfie* and *Diftraction*, its
Caufes, Nature and Effects; the rather

ther becaufe the same has very barrenly been handled, as far as I can learn, by those that have undertaken to treat thereof.

I shall not infist upon the several forts reckoned up by Authors, as *Phrenfie* which they define to be *An Inflamation of the Brain, and its members*, with a continual raving, and sharp conftant Feaver, caufed by cholerick Blood, to which is joyned also excrementious Choler : *Mania*, or *Madnefs*, which is a lofs of the wits, *with raging and fury, but without a Feaver, being a cold and dry Diftemper*, which they say, *arifes from aduft, or burnt-black Choler* ; And *Melancholy*, which is a *doting*, or *Delirium, without a Feaver* (and so different from a Phrenfie) but *with fear and fadnefs* (whereby it differs from madnefs which is accompanied with boldnefs and Fury.)

As all those, and others, varying in Symptoms, are but several *Species*

of

of *Diſtraction*, ſo though *Galen* having conſtituted four *Humors* in the Body, & laid it down for a Principle, that from the exceſs of ſome, or one of them, all Diſeaſes do proceed, and conſequently, was bound to aſſign theſe as cauſes for ſuch Diſtempers; yet more *narrow Searchers* into the *Myſteries of Nature*, have long ſince diſcarded that Doctrine, which ſeems to conſiſt meerly in *Forms* and *Words*, rather then *Reallities*, and do conclude that moſt Diſeaſes ariſe, either from Irregular paſſions of the mind, or poyſonous ferments, occaſioned by ill Dyet, or inproper *Phyſick* in the Body.

§. 2. The truth is, *Madneſs* and *Phrenſie* do generally, and for the moſt part (for ſome other few particular cauſes we ſhall give an account of by and by) ariſe and proceed from various Paſſions and extream Inclinations, as *Love, Hate, Grief,*

Grief, *Covetousness*, *Dispair*, and the like, which do too violently awaken, or stir up the *Central Fires*, or *four first Forms* of the original of Nature, which thereupon do break, forth, violate and destroy the *five inward Senses of the Soul*, whence the outward Senses do arise; So that the Soul loseth its distinguishing property, and then the *Imaginative property* and *Soul's Power* becomes rampant, unbounded, or as it were without a Guide, and consequently such a Soul is unchain'd, or set at liberty from the dark Confinements of the grosser *Senses* and *Reason*, even as men in Dreams; for whatsoever in this state, is represented unto the Soul by the uncontrolable and unbounded Imagination, is essential unto them, whether it be good or evil.

For it is evident that in Madness persons are not deprived of their grosser Senses of the outward Nature, As Seeing, Hearing, Tasting, Smel-

Smelling and Feeling, for those they retain as well as before, but they are bereft of the *inward Senses*, or distinguishments ; and whensoever this happeneth to any, then the Soul is unclothed, and all its Fantasies and Imaginations become as it were substantial unto them, as material things are to those that are in their prefect Senses, and under the Goverment, of Reason.

§. 3. For when any shall forsake, and slight the counsel of the *voice of Wisdom*, and suffer their wills and defires too violently to entertain, and enter into any of the fore-mentioned passions, then presently the *Saturnine* and *Martial* Poysonous Fires are awakened, whence does arise such an Hurley-burley, Confusion, Strife and In-equality between the properties in the *Seven-fold Wheel of Nature*, as will in a moments time subvert the government of the inward Senses and Spirit

Spirit of Wisdom, and puts Reason under Hatches, and all its Faculties into a Tempest and Confusion; so that the Soul is left either without *Pilot* or *Rudder* in this outward sensible World. And being thus deprived of its true Senses, and friendly Guide, or Moderator, viz. *The divine implanted Light*, then the first Forms of the Original nature mutiny, and make War one upon the other, a sullen wrathful property being exasperated, powerfully attracts and endeavours to compass all with a certain *in-drawing Power*, and this is called the *first Form*, or *Saturnine Property*, which gives a Body, or Covering to all Spirits, according to the nature of each Thing or Creature. The second Form is called *Mars*, viz. The high lofty out-going, bitter, fierce fiery Property, which cannot endure to be much holden, or captivated by the attractions and in-drawing Property of *Saturn*,

whence

whence does arife in the Soul a moſt
terrible Conteſt, and annoying Heat;
for the *Saturnine Property* does moſt
powerfully draw *inward*, and endeavour to encompaſs and captivate
all ; but this the fierce high lofty
property and martial bitter Fire
cannot endure, it being contrary
to its Nature ; fo that in this
inteſtine Civil War or Agonous,
State, there is a terrible dark brim-
ſtony or ſulpherous fire generated,
which does fo diſturb all the inward
parts, as if Nature were all on Fire,
even in the Center. The Heart
akes, the inward Body feems to
fwell, and becomes too little for the
Soul, which in this Combuſtion is
fo terribly afflicted, that it will no
longer be confined to the Body and
outward Senfes, but eirher withdraws it felf, and flings up the
Reins of Government, and lets *Reafon*,like a wilde Horfe that hath caſt
off Bit and Bridle, and thrown his
Rider,

Rider, ramble confusedly whither-foever the Imagination shall hurry it; or else fometimes breaks off wholly all Commerce with the Body, and feparates its felf in Indignation, and fo the Life its felf is deftroyed; this being the great and immediate caufe both of Diftraction, and of Hanging, Drowning, and various other forts of *Self-Murder*, which are too frequently commited in the World.

§. 4. The truth is, *Pride* may juftly be faid to be the chief *Procatarick*, or remote original caufe of *Madnefs*; for an abufive Self-flattering Perfwafion, Credulity, or Efteem of Falfhood, do at firft Seduce a perfon into *Prefumption*, and a defpifing of others, or into an Indignation of *Self-Love*, *Anger*, *Hatred*, or Wrathfulnefs, towards his Neighbour; from whence proceeds *Irreligion*, *Unbelief*, *Superftition*, *impenitent*

*impenitent Arrogancy, drunken Di-
sparation,* and *sottish Carelesness.* For
as *Faith* is the Gate unto *Humility,* which is the Truth of the Inte-
lector Understanding, so a credulous
esteem or judgment of Falshood is
the entrance of Presumption and
Arrogancy, and the *first madness of
the Soul.* But other Disturbances,
as *Love, Desire, Sorrow, Fear, Ter-
ror,* &c. are especially stirred up by
extrinsical occasion, and therefore
they do produce their effects, not
only in the Soul, but in the Body
For all passions do in their beginning take away *sleep,* weaken the
Appetite and Digestive Faculties,
and impress *dark Idea's* upon the
Spirits, and at length through a
long immoderate, strong, or sudden
inordinacy, those Idea's do infatu-
ate the *Archeus,* subvert the *Judgment,* and the Soul is, as it were,
shaken out of its place.

S

§. §.

§. 5. Now when the five inward senses of the Soul are weakened or destroyed, then they can no longer present before the Judge the *Thoughts, Imaginations* or *Conceptions,* but they are all formed into *words* as fast as they are generated, there being no controul or room for Judgment to censure what are *fit,* and what are *unfit* to be coyn'd into Expressions: For this cause *Mad People,* and innocent Children, do speak, forth whatever ariseth in their Phantasies; but on the contrary, all those that attain to Maturity of Years, and the knowledge of good and evil, their inward Senses of the Soul being unviolated, especially such as adhere to the counsel of the *Voice of Wisdom,* they let no Conception or Imagination be formed into words before it be presented by the *five Counsellors of the Soul,* before the Judge, which keeps its Court,
and

and Seat of Juftice, in the *Center of Life*; for if this were not more or lefs obferved, would not every man in the world feem to be *Mad*, or Diftracted? For what wild, incoherent, abfurd, ridiculous notions fhould we hear from the moft ferious people, if they fhould continually Speak, and form into words the various Imaginations, and Conceptions that do continually arife from the *Magie* or *Generating Wheel* of the feven *Forms* of *Nature*, which never ftandeth ftill, or ceafeth from working and generating; the Soul of man, and all the Faculties thereof, being a compleat Image of its Creator, *who flumbereth not, nor fleepeth*, but his generative, and wonderful creating power is always active; for never hath any man ceafed from *Imaginations* one quarter an hour in his whole Life, or indeed one moment, no, not even when

when the Body & Sences are afleep,

For though man can ceafe from fpeaking, and may attain the Gift of *Silence*, as any fhall give their wills thereunto, yet they cannot ceafe from *thoughts* and *Conceptions*, either good or evil, according to what property or principle has obtained the government in the Soul ; for if a man could or fhould ceafe from *Imagination*, then alfo he muft of neceffity ceafe from all *Motion* and *Action*, and become an eternal *Stilnefs*, or *Nihilation* ; in which ftate nothing can be brought into Manifeftation, but it muft be done through Motion, Strife and Contention of the Properties ; for all Material and Immaterial were and are brought into Manifeftation firft by Imagination, Defire and Motion ; For the Imagination and the Defire have a moft wonderful deep and hidden Original ; and if its

mighty

mighty property were not captiva-
tĕd, darkned, and as it ere chained in the Clouds of grofs flefh, and
dark Powers of the outward and
corporeal Nature, it would do
wonders.

§. 6. Therefore it is not perhaps
alwayes fo very deplorable an eftate,
as fome fuppofe, to be deprived of
common Senfe and *Reafon* (as they
call it) efpecially, to be a *mad Innocent*. that is, if the property of
Friendlinefs have dominion in the
Soul ; For when men are fo divefted
of their *Rational Faculties*, then
they appear naked, having no *Covering*, *Vail*, or *Figg-leaves* before
them, to hide themfelves in, and
therefore they no longer remain
under a Mask or Difguife, but appear even as they are, which is very
rare to be known in any that retain
their *Senfes* and *Reafon* ; for thofe
two ferve to cover and hide the Con-
S 3   ceptions

ceptions, Thoughts and Imaginations, which continually are generated from the various Properties and
Centers in man, which in innocent
Children, as soon as they have the
use of their Tongues, and in mad
people, is not done, but all Conceptions are promiscuously formed into
words, as they are generated, there
being no Judge nor Councellors to
advise or determine whether they
are fit to be divulged, and Coin'd
into Language, or to be stiffled and
suppressed.

§. 7. The truth is, as the knowledge of evil is man's fall, so if this
sort of *Madness* were practised a-
mongst all men that have the use
of *Reason*, and their *Senses*, it would
be more like *Innocency* and *Christianity*, then most mens general pra-
ctises are now-a-days; I mean, if
every man, laying aside all subtilty
and hypocrisie, would speak his
mind

mind freely to his Neighbour, without Cover or mental Reservations, and leave off speaking of one thing to their neighbour, or Friends faces, and quite other and contrary things behind their backs; To complement persons present, with a thousand *Flatteries* and *Lyes*, and revile the same persons, as soon as they are *absent*, with as many *Calumnies*, *Slanders* and *unjust-Reproaches*, which is one of the worst kinds of *Madness*, and indeed a Devilish one, because they know they do not as they ought, being at that very time accused and condemned by the *Voice of Wisdom*, or divine Principle; nor is there scarce one thing in Ten that men in the World do act, but is far greater *Madness* and Evil, than those things which persons do that are deprived of their *Sences*.

For Example; Is it not a greater Extravagance for an Ambitious man to sell his Liberty, and became a

slave

slave to the Lusts and Capricio's of *Grandees,* to spend whole years in supple Attendances, Crouching, Cringing Fawning or Dissembling, only in hopes of being one day made a *great man,* or having an airey Title added (like a Rattle) to his name, and seeing people stand Cap in hand to him, whom he imagines to *admire him,* though in truth as many of them as are wise, deride and pitty his egregious Folly? For a Lascivious man to waste his Wealth, his Strength, and expose both Body and Soul, for the filthy imbraces of a loathsom Strumpet? And hazard his Life and honour in attempting the Chastity of some virtuous Woman, and be ready to dye for the Love of her, whom as soon as he has debaucht, he will scorn and hate? For men to swallow down vast Estates at their *Throats,* and Piss away the Labours of their Ancestors against the *Walls.* To load
their

their Table with variety of Dishes, and be at any charge for *poinant Sawces*, to provoke the Appetite beyond the power, as well as necessities of Nature, that their Bodies may be filled with *Diseases?* That they may roar under the *Stone*, and the *Illiaac Passion*, and live Tormented Lives, and dye an Immature Death? For Parents to cark, and care, and vex, and torment themselves with unreasonable Toils, and many times hazard their *Souls*, for unjust Gain, meerly, to heap up Estates for their Children, who all ready wish them dead ; or to leave Riches amongst strangers, who in their frolicks laugh at the memory of the *old Miser*, and make themselves and their Companions merry with telling ridiculous Stories of him, who for their sakes, and for the getting those very Houses, and those Bowls they carouze in, lieb perhaps broyling in the hottest Caverns

verns of the Everlasting Tophet?

These, and an hundred the like things, which are the main business, and the daily imployment of many, that would be counted the shrewdest and most notable part of Mankind: Are not, I say, all these far greater, and more mischievous *Phrensies*,than for a man to pull of his Garments, and sit naked, and spend time in weaving of *Straws* or *Building* with Chalk upon the Walls innumerable Cities, whereof he fancies himself to be Emperor? To speak Truth, the World is but a great *Bedlam*, where those that are *more mad*, lock up those that are *lofs*; the *first* presumptuously, and knowingly, committing Evils both against God their Neighbours and themselves; but the *last*, not knowing what they do, are as it were next door to *innocency*, especially when the Evil Properties were not awakened, nor predominant in the Complexion in the

time

time of their Senſes: Tell me I pray?
Are not all theſe Intemperances, Violence, Oppreſſion, Murder and ſavage
Evils, and Superfluities deſervedly
to be accounted the worſt Effects
of Madneſs? As alſo, Lying,
Swearing, vain Imaginations, and
living in and under the power of
evil Spirits, more to be dreaded
than the condition of thoſe that
want the uſe of Senſes and Reaſon;
and therefore are eſteemed Mad?

§. 8. As for the *Species of Mad-*
neſs they are as *various* as men are
in their Complexions; for according to what Principle and property, whether good or evil, does govern the Life, in the time of their
retaining their Reaſon and Senſes,
ſuch a property does more clearly
manifeſt it ſelf when the Reaſon
and Senſes are broken to pieces;
for this cauſe, ſome who have ſeem-
ed very Religious, and ſoberly in-
clined

clined, as long as they retain'd their Senses and outward Reason, as soon as they become deprived thereof, the bitter envious fierce wrathful proud Spirit appears in its own form, and has its operation without let or hindrance, which was before by the cunning Reason and sensual subtilty kept in, that it could not manifest it self; for some men have obtain'd so much outward government over this bitter Spirit, that they can at one and the same time cry *Hosanna*, and *Crucifie*; say, *God bless you*, and in their hearts wish your *destruction*: But when such people, who hide their *Woolvish* and *Bearish Natures*, in the external sheeps cloathing of a dissembled Innocency, happen to be *Mad* or deprived of outward Sense and natural Reason, then they discover the Savage Nature that ruled before in the Center of their Souls. But others, who in the time of their sound Senses, were

accounted

accounted harſh and moroſs, or ſe-
vere, their Tongues not ſo ſmoothly
plain'd, or Tipt with Complements,
but yet their words and works more
agreeable to their inſides; that is,
they *ſpeak* as they *think*, and do not
play the Hypocrites, by retaining ſubtil Reſervations, or ſaying
one thing, and at the ſame time re-
ſolving on another; ſuch, I ſay,
though many of them did not ſeem
to be ſo fair and good men as the
former, yet they are really more innocent, and have far better Principles within, than the others, who
made uſe of their Natural Faculties,
to hide and cover the ſubtil bitter
Spirit; and therefore when theſe
latter plain ſort of people happen to
be diſtracted, they appear more calm
and friendly than the former, be-
cauſe the good property had a greater dominion in the Soul.

§. 9. Every perſon when diſtur-
bed

bed in his Senses and Reason, then the distinguishing Faculties of Nature does variously appear in properties and Qualities, differing according to which of the seven Forms Nature did carry the upper dominion in the Complexion. Therefore *Mad People* vary as much in their inclinations and passions of *Love* and *Hate* as they did when in their Senses.

For Example; If the first, or *Saturnine* Property did preside in the Soul, and be not corrected, moderated, allayed, and made friendly by *Wisdoms Voice*, whilst they remained in their Senses, then such will manifest themselves when *Mad*, in sullen, dogged, mischievous Melancholy dispositions and Inclinations, with Blasphemous words, apt to hurt, and be injurious, with *Sour* evil Complexion and Looks.

But if the *Jovial Properties* had the uppermost Governments in the time of

of their Reafon, then fuch, when
out of their wits, are for the moft
part affable and friendly, ufing no
cruel words, nor fo apt to do hurt, or
be churlifh, or dogged.

But if the *Martial Property* be fu-
perior in the Complexion, fuch
when deprived of Senfe and Reafon,
become *furious*, *blafphemous*, apt to
all mifchief and violence, great Swea-
rers, and very unruly, fierce, turbu-
lent, and raging.

But if the *Solar Property* do bare
Rule, fuch have great and high
thoughts, and lofty ¦maginations,
fancying themfelves to be *Kings* and
Princes, and that all are in fubjection
to them; and between while, they
are very unruly fierce and boifterous,
when they think they are not re-
fpected or humoured according to
that Quality they have affumed to
themfelves.

So where the *Venereal Property*
fwayes in the Complexion fuch are
between

between whiles friendly, apt to
laugh, and be merry, often discoursing of Love affairs, and will sing
and dance, but sometimes are little
out-ragious, though not like the
former; for these people seldom do
any hurt, nor are they subject to
Cursing Swearing, or such like evil
Speaking.

Where the *Property* of *Mercury*
does bear sway in the constitution,
there is a strange mixture of Imaginations, they are apt to think themselves very cunning, extraordinary
free, and frolicksom, with their
Tongues running out of one thing
into another, prone always to talk
too much, and very furious bold and
raging, but calm at certain Intervals.

Lastly, where the *Lunar property*
predominates, such people are ex-
treamly unconstant, fierce, and raving, never at any certainty, but
roaming out of one thing into another

ther: And not only this laft fort, but all other *Mad people* are better or worfe, according to the Moti-ons, Influences, Configurations and Afpects of the Cœleftials, and their benevolent or malevolent Rayes, towards the Ruling Conftellation of each mans Complexion, becaufe all people that are deprived of the ufe of their Reafon, Senfe and diftin-guifhing Faculties, are more imme-diately fubjected to the outward-moft Government and Influences of the Stars and Elements. And you may perceive a fenfible alteration in their Humours, Difpofitions and Inclinations, as the Cœleftials alter; which as they have Influence upon, and do vary and change all things, fo more efpecially do they opperate upon thofe that have loft the gui-dance of the *Will*, which is the *Pri-mum Mobile* of mans Life: There-fore it is obferved, that diftracted

T. people

people are more subject to be alter-
ed by the Influences Cœleſtial, e-
ſpecially by the progreſs and Configurations, that the *Moon* has
with the other *Erraticks* and Con-
ſtellations, ſhe being the Manſion-
houſe or *Magazine*, which receives
all the Influences of the greater
and higher Bodies, or Stars: And
therefore perſons bereaved of their
Wits, are in our Engliſh Laws
called *Lunaticks*, from the great
power ſhe hath upon ſuch people.

§. 10. By Cuſtom, Senſe and
Reaſon, moſt men do hide their
inward Inclinations, Diſpoſitions
Complexions, and what property
carries the upper dominion in their
Hearts and Souls, ſo that the ſame
may by ſeveral means be diſcover-
ed and laid open, is manifeſt in
Drunkenneſs, which is a kind of
ſhort

short *Phrensie*, or *Temporary Madness*, which make people appears
in various *Moods* and *Dispositions*;
for those that seemed of a *Malancholy Complexion*, seem *Sanguine*;
and the *Sanguine, Malancholy*; for it
renders men to be that outwardly
which they are inwardly; for this
cause, some that are counted, and
seem to most men to be *Severe* and
Austere; when drink has opened
the *Sanguine Gate of Nature*, are
found to be very familiar, friendly
and kind in their words and works:
But on others, it hath a quite contrary operation, *viz.* such who
carried themselves very affable and
friendly, when overcome with *Liquor*, grow Cruel, Quarrelsom,
Devilish and Uncivil, which does
clearly intimate, that the *Saturnine*
and *Martial* Principles did predominate in the Soul; for drink makes
people appear in various Forms,

because

because during the operation thereof, they are really deprived of the
Exercise of their Right *Reason* and
Sences of true *distinguishments* of
things, whereby they are uncover-
ed, and as it were left naked (as
Noah was, after he had drank too
liberally of the fruit of his new
planted Vines) And so the inside
appears as it is, in its own *Form*
and *Nature*, which does most truly
discover the Complexion and natural Inclinations; and what property does govern essentially in a
man; for then all glosses and cunning are removed; whereas whilst
a man is *himself* (as they use to call
it) Shame, Reason and good Breed-
ing put a Restraint upon those viti-
ous Inclinations, lurking within
and suffer them not to appear;
but when they are deprived of their
Sences and Reason, then they have
no power to use those subtil Arts
of

of *Hypocrifie*, but what form foever
has the predominancy does difplay
and manifeft it felf in its own Co-
lours. And therefore as foon as
they recover their Reafon, and
come to their Senfes, they are a-
fhamed of what they did, and by
Reafon, and Breding, endeavour
to hide thefe Defects and Ill Qualities, which rule over them. And
thus not a few through *Wit* and
Subtilty appear as if they were Saints,
but in truth they remain but little
better than *Devils*; fo great is the
power of mans Wit and contrived
Underftanding that he can appear
with two faces to deceive others
firft, and himfelf at laft : It is
therefore a very difficult matter for
any to judge of mens Complexions, or real Inclinations, except God
have endued him with fomewhat
of the univerfal underftanding of
the nature of things, and of the

signatures of nature; for the form or figure of each thing, does to the enlightened Eye discover the inward Properties thereof.

But this is more evidently discovered in *Phrensy* or *Madness*, the same being a real turning of the inside of all the natural Properties and Faculties of the Soul outward; so that whatever mad people do externally in words or actions, the very same other Folk do inwardly in thoughts and Imaginations; and the difference is only this; The one speaks and forms every thought into words: having not the Bridle of sense nor Reason to restrain him; the other often times cuts off such and such thoughts and Imaginations in the Budd, or at least shuts the grand Gate, the *Mouth*, and keeps those shameful unruly Stragglers in, not suffering the Organs and Properties of

Nature

Nature to form them into Articular Expreſſions.

§. 11. It is alſo further to be noted that all, or moſt *Mad People*, are far ſtronger, and more able to endure Hardſhip, Hunger, Cold, and the like inconveniences, although many of them are naturally of weak *tender* natures, and during the continuances of their Senſes, and Reaſoning Vigour, did indulge and enure themſelves to tenderneſs; yet when once they become Mad, they are ſo ſtrong and powerful, that ſome of them muſt have two, three or four men to hold and rule them; and as to their enduring of Cold, it is wonderful, for even nice, tender Gentlewomen, who Screen themſelves all the Winter by luſty Fires, in warm Beds, and cloſe Chambers, and the like; with choice Foods,

and

and cordial Drink, are no sooner
deprived of their Reason and Senfes, but they leap over all these
things, and endure hardship, to ad-
miration, without prejudice to
their health, even beyond the stur-
diest constitution; the reason whereof is, because when people, by any
of the fore-mentioned, Accidents,
and Passions, fall into Distraction,
the whole Syftime of Nature being
put into a tumultuous unequal Motion, the same does in a moment of
time rouse up or awaken the deep
or great Original Fierce, Poysonous
Fire ; or the four first Forms
of Nature. Now when these tur-
bulent Fires of *Saturn* and *Mars*
have obtained the dominion, and
idle Government in the Soul,
they with a rapid motion deftroy
the Government of the *Divine
Light*, and also of the *humane Nature*, which are and ought to be
the

the *Moderator*, and *Allayers* of the
aforeſaid original poyſonous Fire,
and the true Diſtinguiſhers between
what is good, and the contrary,
and thus the Spirit being alwayes
as upon a *ferment*, and uncontrolable motion, it warms, ſtrengthens,
and oftentimes does as it were put
a new life into the very Element
of the Body, whence a ſtrong vi-
gerous ſtrength and agility of body, and a Defence of Cold, *Hun-*
ger, and the like inconveniences does
proceed.

This is further demonſtrated by
all ſorts of people in *Paſsion*, of
either Love or Hate, or when ſur-
priſed, or in *Sudden Frights*, are
they not Generally under ſuch
Circumſtances of far greater Spirit,
ſtronger and more active Bodies,
and rendered more able to *Lift*, *Run*,
Carry, *Fight*, or any other thing
Good or Evil, then at other times,
and

and have aboundantly more courage, and they can attempt and perform many wonderful things without the leaft fufpition of Danger, which at other times they tremble think of, and would not for the greateft rewards be prefwaded to undertake.

Nay, when the Soul-Fires are kindled in the poyfonous Root, a man can whithout Dread and Fear lay violent hands on himfelf, fo wonderfully great is its power, for this is a madnefs of the higheft degree, fince *no man*, (as the Apoftle faid) *hates his own Flefh, but loveth and cherifhes it*, which ought well to be confidered by all Jurors concerned in fuch cafes.

So likewife when men are overcome with *Drink*, the fpirituous Properties of the ftrong Liquor, received in too great a quantity, do by *Simily* incorporate with the

Spirits

Spirits of Nature, in the Elements of the Body, so that it inkindles the Original fierce Fires, and puts the whole Frame of Nature into a tumultuous state of Inequality, and during its operation, *Reason* it captivated; and men in this condition may truly be said to be in the worst kind of *Madness*, as clearly is manifested by their idle leud Discourses, and mischievious Actions.

Likewise *Malancholy* people, when grievously oppressed with its taciturne Properties, are in a degree deprived of their natural Sences and Reason, and the Soul becomes as it were *Spiritual*, so that it Imagines, Sees, Hears, and Apprehends wonderful things, which, though to others appear as meer fansies, yet to them are real, and *essential*.

§ 12.

§. 12. As for the *Original Seed*, or Spring of Phrensies or Madness in the Body, it must be noted, besides what hath been already said, that there is in the Pipe of the Artery of the *Stomach*, a vital Faculty of the Soul, for the in-beaming of Rayes of Light into the *Heart*, so long as it is in a good state, but when through Passions and Disorders it behaveth it self rashly, or amiss, then presently Heart-burning, Fainting, Giddiness of the Head, Appoplexes, Epilexsies, Drousie-Evils, Watchings, Madnesses, Head-akes, Convultions, &c. by the means we have herein before described are sturred up. And since the stomach is the Seat of the Concupiscible Faculty; and from whose fumes both sleep and watchings are occationed; and since that *Alienation of mind*

mind chiefly proceeds from irregu-
ler defire, it may rationally be con-
cluded, that the Prime *local Spring*,
or Seed of Madnefs is in or near
the ftomach, or its neighbouring
parts, the *Midriff and the Spleen*;
though afterwards it difplays its
male-influences upon the *Brain*; for
a man forms his Images in the
Midriff; as well thofe of the *Concu-
pifcible*, or Defiring, as thofe of the
Irafcible, or Wrathful Faculty,
fo that Madnefs is therefore not
undefervedly called, *Hipocondria-
cal*; for the prime Efficacy of di-
fturbances confifteth in the *Spleen*,
and therefore perhaps Antiquity
hath counted *Saturn* the principle of
the Starry power, and higheft of
the wandering Stars, to wit, that
which fhould caft his influence
downwards on the reft, but that
the reft fhould in no wife reflect
upwards, becaufe they are believed
to

to conspire for the Commodities of sublunary things, but not on the contrary upwards; and therefore, though they called the same *Saturn*, the Original of Life, and beginning of Conceptions, or Generations, yet they also named him, The *Devourer* of his own *young Children*, as thereby intimating, that as the *Images* or Ideas framed by the *desirable* Faculty do make Seed fruitfull, so also the Inns of Digestion in us, when they are exorbitant, consume the new and tender *Blood*, and bring many *Diseases* upon us.

§. 13. But besides the before-mentioned most usual Causes of *Madness*, from the *Passions*, we deny not but sometimes other things received in from without, may occasion *alienation* of *Mind*.

Thus the Biting of a Mad-Dog
con veys

conveys a Venom impregnated with its own raging Idea, which is soon communicated to the Spirit of man, and produces in him that wilde foolish conceit, called, by Phyſitians *Hydrophobia*, or a fear of Water, in which the Perſon affected by an error of his imaginations ſeems to ſee the Image of a *Dog*; and in time, if no Remedy be found, grows raving Mad, and dies, ſo alſo thoſe that are Bit with the *Tarantula*, a venomous Beaſt, or Inſect, ſeen ſometimes in *Italy*, and other forraign Parts) are particularly diſpoſed to a certain kind of skipping or *Dancing* Phrenſie, which at laſt proves Mortal: So ſome by ignorance of Apothecaries, who have taken *Henbane*-Seed inſteed of *Dill*, have immediately become Mad, Stupid and Fooliſh, ſo that they could not utter an intelligible word, for all which there are

are distinct Reasons in Nature, but too tedious here to be related, and somewhat unnecessary, because these Cases very rarely occur amongst us.

§. 14. As to the Cure of Madness in general, the Schools commonly prescribe *Blood-letting*, and *Sleep-procuring Medicines*, but with how much success daily experience witnesseth, they mistake the *Cause*, and therefore blindly combat with the *Effect*; and for the latter, let such as intend to cure Distractions by *sleepyfing* things, take notice that *stupifactive Medicines* do scarce procure sleep unto mad persons by a four-fold Dose; and when all is done, they increase the *Madness*; for *Madness* is nothing but an *Erring Sleepifying Power*, because every Madman dreameth waking; and therefore *Stupefactive Dreams* are

are thereby added unto *doting
Dreams* in waking, and so the mind
more disturbed then before. Therefore undoubtedly, the sealing Character in a Madman, presupposes
a restoring of the hurt reason,
and a correction of the Poyson by
its Antidote, but not another stupefactive Poyson to be added unto it.

And as Supifying Medicines are
of little value, but rather prejudi-
cial, so, much more mischievous
is too much Company, and pra-
ting, and especially, the Teazing
of such distempered People with
unnecessary Questions; on which
score, as I must acknowledge that
Gallant Structure of *New Bethlam*
to be one of the Prime Ornaments
of the City of *London*, and a No-
ble Monument of *Charity*, so I
would with all Humility beg the
Honorable and worthy Governours
U thereof:

thereof, that they would be plea-
ed to ufe fome Effectual means,
for reftraining their inferior Offi-
cers, from admitting fuch Swarms
of People, of all Ages and De-
grees, for only a little paltry Profit
to come. in there, and with their
noife, and vain queftions to difturb
the poor Souls; as efpecially fuch,
as do Refort thither on Holy-dayes,
and fuch fpare time, when for fe-
veral hours (almoft all day long)
they can never be at any quiet, for
thofe inportunate Vifitants, whence
manifold great inconveniences do a-
rife. For,

Firft, Tis a very Undecent, In-
humane thing to make, as it
were, a *Show* of thofe Unhappy
Objects of *Charity* committed to
their Care, (by expofing them,
and making too perhapes of either
Sexs) to the Idle Curiofity of e-
very vain Boy, petulant Wench,
or

or Drunken Companion, going
along from one Apartment to the
other, and Crying out; This
Woman is in for Love; That Man
for Jealousie; He has Over-studied
himself, and the Like.

Secondly, This staring Rabble
seldom fail of asking more then an
hundred impertinent Questions. ──
As, what are you here for? How
Long have you been here, &c.
which most times enrages the
Distracted person, tho calme and
quiet before, and then the poor
Creature falls a Raving, and too
probably, a Cursing and Swearing,
and so the holy, and tremendous
name of God is dishonored, whi'est
the wicked people, who think it
a rare Diversion, instead of Trem-
bling, as indeed they ought, being themselves really Guilty, as
the Occasion of all these Blasphe-
mies, fall a Laughing and Hoot-
ing

ing, and so the poor distracted
Creatures become twice more fierce
and violent then ever.

Thirdly, As long as such Disturbances are suffered, there is little
Hope that any Cure or Medicine
should do them good to reduce
them to their Senses or right Minds,
as we call it, and so the very Principle end of the House is defeated.
Certainly the most hopeful means
towards their Recovery would be
to keep them with a Clean Spare
Diet, and as quiet as may be, and
to let none come at them but their
particular Friends, Grave sober
People and such as they have a
kindness for, and those to, not
alwayes, but only at proper times,
whereby discoursing with them in
their Lused intervals Gravely, So-
berly, and Discreetly, and humour-
ing them in little things, shall do
much more, I am Confident, toward

ward their Cure, then moſt of the
Medicines that are commonly Ad-
miniſtred ; But to come home to
the Cure we muſt Conſider that a
mad Idea, imprinted on the principles of Life, cannot be taken a-
way, but together with the Subject
that hath cloſed it ; therefore a Remedy is to be found out, which may
Slay, take away, or obliterate that
Image of madneſs, or the Blot ſo
characterized ; juſt, as 'tis ſaid, a
Blemiſh imprinted by the *longing
Mother*, doth by the moving of the
hand of a dead *Carcaſe* (that was
killed by a lingering Conſumpti-
on) on it, until the cold thereof
ſhall pierce the Blemiſhed part, va-
niſh away for the future of its own
accord.

After the ſame manner the Idea
of madneſs ought to be put to
flight, whether it be done by the
death of the ſaid Idea, or by in-
generating

generating an Idea of equal pre-
vailency, or one that over-power-
eth the foolish Idea; for from
hence it comes' to pass, that a remedy for Madness hath hitherto
been dispaired of, because the nature and properties of the Distemper hath not been searched for beyond the excesses of *first Qualities.* Nor can it be but the scope
of curing must be difficult, because not only the Idea of a cor-
rupted imagination, and a *fealy-
mark* and blemish is introduced into the innermost point of the understanding, but' also, because the
restoring of the *inbred Spirit* is
hardly to be effected, since the
sweet Government of the *divine
Principle* is cast of, and the Creature is now no longer able to turn
his *Will* thereunto, or to hearken
unto the *Voice* of *Wisdom* for help;
but *Infinite Goodness* is never wanting

ting to thofe that truly feek him in
Humility, that with Bowels of *Charity* towards their Neighbour ; to
fuch God, the Giver of every good
and perfe&t Gift, will in his own
due time reveal and communicate
a *proper* Remedy ; for Medicines
have with a fuccefs been admini-
ftred wherein a *Symbole*, or Mark
of Refemblance doth inhabite ;
that is the firmental imaginations of a founder judgment. For
truly, as there are Poyfons of the
Mind, caufing the allienations
thereof, for fometimes, or for
the whole fpace of Life ; to wit,
fuch as do introduce a proper
Phantafie into us, as a *Mad Dog*,
the *Tarantula*, &c. So alfo there
are in *fimples* their own Fruits, of
the knowledge of Good and Evil,
in their firft face indeed *poyfonous*,
under which notwithftanding the
more

more rich Treasures, and renewings of the *mind* are kept.

The Antients Celebrated even to a proverb, the vertues of *black Hellebore* in such cases; For although manifold *Vomitive* Medicines are not wanting, yet a peculier vertue is attributed to *Hellibore*, for a *Mad brain*; not that the poysonous and hurtful qualities doth reach unto the *Head*, but because it unloads the *Midriff* and the *Spleen*, the original Seats of this distemper, and so by consequence relieves the *Brain*, which was affected by a secondary Passion.

§. 15. For such as have been *Bitten* with a *Mad Dog*, the Dutch (as I have heard) do prevent the Mischief, by applying to the place a raw Herring salted, for three

three dayes fpace, every day re-
newed ; but if that had been neg-
lected, and the party begins to
dote, and fear the water, (which
is one of the firft fymtoms of that
kind of Diftraction) then they
get him on fhip board, ftrip him,
and tye him to the end of the
Sail-yard, and lifting him firft on
high, *plung him down headlong into the Sea*, and let him remain a
little while under water, and fo
a fecond, and third time and then
take him down, place him on a
fmooth place with his back upwards, and his head declining,
or as it were hanging over fome-
thing, and fo will caft up all the
water received into his ftomach,
and thence forward be perfectly
cured.

And *Vanhelmont* witneffes, that
fuch plunging over head and ears

is

is a *Cure*, not only in that case, but in *other* inveterate *Mania's* or *Madnesses*, and in fresh water as well in the Sea ; He sayes, he hath often tryed it, and was never deceived in the event, but when through fear of drowning them, he drew the *Mad* persons too soon from under the water.

For *prevention* of these *distracted Calamities*, since generally, and most commonly they proceed from excess of *Passion*, and irregular *Desire* ; Therefore let all Persons Study by Temperance, and Moderating their Affections, to eschew those baneful Evils, and by hearkening to the *Voyce* of *Wisdom*, they shall assuredly avoid them ; and many other Distempers and Mischiefs : Therefore, O Man ! consider what is before mentioned, keep thy Self to thy Self ;

turn

turn thy Eye of thy Underftanding *inward*; obferve thy *own Center*, and learn to underftand with
David, *That thou art Fearfully and
Wonderfully made*, and fo by the
Conduct and Guidance of the Divine Light and Love thou fhalt
come to know the wonderfull Power of God in thy own Soul, which
will open unto thee both the Myfte-
ries of *Nature*, and the Treafures of
Eternity.

FINIS

ERRATA.

Page 2. Line 6. for pithy Read pitchy. l. 21. r. Read.
p. 29. l. 8. r. Eviternal. p. 30. l. 23. r. form. p. 35.
l. 22. r. Procatartick. p. 44. l. 6. r. Offices. p. 47.
l. 17. r. Emanations. p. 48. l. 6. dele its. p. 67. l. 12. r.
Analogy. p. 69. l. 7. dele the point at Affections. l. 16. r. its
felf. p. 148. l. 24. r. Sanative. p. 151. l. 24. r. *Cacodemon*
p. 157. l. 22. r. forward. p. 162. l. 22. r. why fhould. p.
163. l. 20. dele Spirits of. p. 170. l. 18. f. *Indination* r. *Indignation.* p. 183. l. 13 f. its r. this. p. 186. l. 12. f. prety
r. petty. p. 192. l. 21. f. depraved r. deprived. p. 200.
l. 15. r. were the. p. 204. l. 20. r. irradiations. p. 220.
l. 6. r. in fome meafure. p. 221. l. 12. r. immerfed. p. 225.
l. 4. r. Oppofition. p. 226. l. 4. r. If thofe Inquirers. p. 229.
l. 4. r. Spirits. p. 232. l. 6. r. Hermes. p. 244. l. 6, 7. f.
underftanding r. underftand. p. 250. l. 8, 9. r. *membranes.*
p. 256. l. 14, 15. r. *Procatartick.* l. 19, 20. f. Indignation
r. Imagination. p. 260. l. 19. after Immaterial add things.
p. 256. l. 17. f. *lofs* r. *lefs.* p. 290. l. 22. f. making r. method. p. 295. l. 2. r. and with.